Anyone who hears these words of mine and obeys them is like a wise man who built his house on a rock. The rain poured down, the rivers overflowed, and the wind blew against that house. But it did not fall because it was built on rock.

But anyone who hears these words of mine and does not obey them is like a foolish man who built his house on sand. The rain poured down, the rivers overflowed, the wind blew hard against that house, and it fell. And what a terrible fall that was!

Matthew 7

THE LIFE AND WORDS OF
JESUS

Compiled by Pat Alexander

1817

HARPER & ROW, PUBLISHERS, SAN FRANCISCO

Cambridge, Hagerstown, New York, Philadelphia,
London, Mexico City, São Paulo, Sydney

Acknowledgements
Photographs: Lion Publishing/David
Alexander.
Bible quotations, by permission of the copyright
holders: *Good News Bible,* the Bible in
Today's English Version. Copyright © American
Bible Society, 1976. Used by permission.

Printed in Spain

FIRST U.S. EDITION

**Library of Congress Cataloging in Publication
Data**
Bible. N.T. Gospels. English. Today's English.
  Selections. 1983.
    THE LIFE AND WORDS OF JESUS.

  1. Jesus Christ – Biography – Sources, Biblical.
2. Jesus Christ – Words. 3. Christian biography –
Palestine. I. Alexander, Pat, 1937– . II. Title.
BS2553.T55A43 1983   226'.052   83-47715
ISBN 0-06-065255-1

83   84   85   86   87   10   9   8   7   6   5   4   3   2   1

CONTENTS

A WAITING WORLD

The world 2,000 years ago, like our world today, was looking for salvation. For some, this was a yearning for God to visit his people, to set them free, to introduce a way of peace. For others it was a cry for justice, for deliverance from the cruel Roman occupation, a cry for revolution. Others again were looking for personal fulfilment. The old pagan religions were bankrupt. The cults and superstitions could offer only escapism, not true satisfaction.

The world was looking for a Messiah, a saviour – the one whose coming the prophets had predicted . . .

The people that walked in darkness
have seen a great light:
they that dwell in the land
of the shadow of death,
upon them hath the light shined . . .
For unto us a child is born,
unto us a son is given:
and the government shall be
upon his shoulder:
and his name shall be called Wonderful,
Counseller, The mighty God,
The everlasting Father,
The Prince of Peace.
Isaiah 9

As in our own day, Jerusalem at the time of the birth of Jesus was a centre of political intrigue and religious rivalry.

Prologue to John's Gospel

In the beginning was the Word,
and the Word was with God,
and the Word was God.
The same was in the beginning with God.
All things were made by him;
and without him was not anything made
that was made.
In him was life;
and the life was the light of men.
And the light shineth in darkness;
and the darkness comprehended it not . . .
That was the true Light, which lighteth
every man that cometh into the world.
He was in the world,
and the world was made by him,
and the world knew him not.

He came unto his own,
and his own received him not.
But as many as received him,
to them gave he power to become
the sons of God,
even to them that believe on his name:
Which were born, not of blood,
nor of the will of the flesh,
nor of the will of man, but of God.
And the Word was made flesh, and dwelt
among us,
(and we beheld his glory,
the glory as of the only begotten
of the Father,)
full of grace and truth.

John 1

The Angel's Message

God's message was to come,
not by someone high and mighty,
but through an ordinary couple.
Mary was engaged to Joseph,
a carpenter, in the provincial town
of Nazareth, in Palestine,
a far-off corner of the Roman Empire.

God sent the angel Gabriel to a town in Galilee named Nazareth. He had a message for a girl promised in marriage to a man named Joseph, who was a descendant of King David. The girl's name was Mary.

The angel came to her and said, 'Peace be with you! The Lord is with you and has greatly blessed you!'

Mary was deeply troubled by the angel's message, and she wondered what his words meant.

The angel said to her, 'Don't be afraid, Mary; God has been gracious to you. You will become pregnant and give birth to a son, and you will name him Jesus. He will be great and will be called the Son of the Most High God. The Lord God will make him a king, as his ancestor David was, and he will be the king of the descendants of Jacob for ever; his kingdom will never end!'

Mary said to the angel, 'I am a virgin. How, then, can this be?'

The angel answered, 'The Holy Spirit will come on you, and God's power will rest upon you. For this reason the holy child will be called the Son of God. Remember your relative Elizabeth. It is said that she cannot have children, but she herself is now six months pregnant, even though she is very

old. For there is nothing that God cannot do.'

'I am the Lord's servant,' said Mary; 'may it happen to me as you have said.'

And the angel left her.

Luke 1

Cupped in the hills of Galilee, Nazareth was a small, busy provincial town. It seemed just too ordinary for the events that were to take place there . . .

Mary's song
The Magnificat

**My soul doth magnify the Lord,
And my spirit hath rejoiced
in God my Saviour.
For he hath regarded the low estate
of his handmaiden:
for, behold, from henceforth
all generations shall call me blessed.
For he that is mighty hath done
to me great things;
and holy is his name.
And his mercy is on them that fear him
from generation to generation.
He hath shewed strength with his arm;
he hath scattered the proud
in the imagination of their hearts.
He hath put down the mighty
from their seats,
and exalted them of low degree.
He hath filled the hungry
with good things;
and the rich he hath sent empty away.
He hath holpen his servant Israel,
in remembrance of his mercy;
As he spake to our fathers,
to Abraham, and to his seed for ever.**

Luke 1

No Room at the Inn

Mary's secret was shared with Joseph.
And God confirmed in a dream his special
purpose for this child. Jesus was
to 'save his people from their sins'.
He was the fulfilment of Isaiah's
ancient prophecy, 'Behold, a virgin
shall be with child, and shall bring
forth a son, and they shall call
his name Emmanuel, "God with us".'
Then the Roman Emperor ordered a census.
Everyone went to his own town, to register.
So, with the baby almost due,
Mary and Joseph set out for Bethlehem,
the birthplace of King David,
because Joseph was a descendant of
David . . .

And while they were in Bethlehem, the time came for her to have her baby. She gave birth to her first son, wrapped him in strips of cloth and laid him in a manger – there was no room for them to stay in the inn.

There were some shepherds in that part of the country who were spending the night in the fields, taking care of their flocks. An angel of the Lord appeared to them, and the glory of the Lord shone over them.

They were terribly afraid, but the angel said to them, 'Don't be afraid! I am here with good news for you, which will bring great joy to all the people. This very day in David's town your Saviour was born – Christ the Lord! And this is what will prove it to you: you will find a baby wrapped in strips of cloth and lying in a manger.'

Suddenly a great army of heaven's angels appeared with the angel, singing praises to God:

'Glory to God in the highest heaven,
and peace on earth to those with whom he is pleased!'

When the angels went away from them back into heaven, the shepherds said to one another, 'Let's go to Bethlehem and see this thing that has happened, which the Lord has told us.'

So they hurried off and found Mary and Joseph and saw the baby lying in the manger. When the shepherds saw him, they told them what the angel had said about the child. All who heard it were amazed at what the shepherds said. Mary remembered all these things and thought deeply about them. The shepherds went back, singing praises to God for all they had heard and seen; it had been just as the angel had told them.

The time came for Joseph and Mary to perform the ceremony of purification, as the Law of Moses commanded. So they took the child to Jerusalem to present him to the Lord . . .

At that time there was a man named Simeon living in Jerusalem. He was a good, devout man and was waiting for Israel to be saved. The Holy Spirit was with him and had assured him that he would not die before he had seen the Lord's promised Messiah. Led by the Spirit, Simeon went into the Temple. When the parents brought the child Jesus into the Temple to do for him what the Law required, Simeon took the child in his arms and gave thanks to God.

Luke 2

Shepherd boys still watch their flocks on the rocky terraces surrounding the town of Bethlehem; and in the ancient temple area of Jerusalem the religious meet to pray and meditate.

Simeon's prayer
The Nunc Dimittis

Lord, now lettest thou thy servant
depart in peace,
according to thy word:
For mine eyes have seen thy salvation,
Which thou hast prepared
before the face of all people;
A light to lighten the Gentiles,
and the glory of thy people Israel.
Luke 2

STAR IN THE EAST

Soon afterwards, some men who studied the stars came from the east to Jerusalem and asked, 'Where is the baby born to be the king of the Jews? We saw his star when it came up in the east, and we have come to worship him.'

When King Herod heard about this, he was very upset, and so was everyone else in Jerusalem. He called together all the chief priests and the teachers of the Law and asked them, 'Where will the Messiah be born?'

'In the town of Bethlehem in Judaea,' they answered. 'For this is what the prophet wrote:

"Bethlehem in the land of Judah,
you are by no means the least
of the leading cities of Judah;
for from you will come a leader
who will guide my people Israel." '

So Herod called the visitors from the east to a secret meeting and found out from them the exact time the star had appeared. Then he sent them to Bethlehem with these instructions:

'Go and make a careful search for the child, and when you find him, let me know, so that I too may go and worship him.'

And so they left, and on their way they saw the same star they had seen in the east. When they saw it, how happy they were, what joy was theirs! It went ahead of them until it stopped over the place where the child was. They went into the house, and when they saw the child with his mother Mary, they knelt down and worshipped him. They brought out their gifts of gold, frankincense, and myrrh, and presented them to him.

Then they returned to their country by another road, since God had warned them in a dream not to go back to Herod.

After they had left, an angel of the Lord appeared in a dream to Joseph and said, 'Herod will be looking for the child in order to kill him. So get up, take the child and his mother and escape to Egypt, and stay there until I tell you to leave.'

Joseph got up, took the child and his mother, and left during the night for Egypt, where he stayed until Herod died.
Matthew 2

Like Mary, a young mother in Bethlehem today wraps her baby against the chill winds (TOP). The Church of the Nativity (RIGHT) is built on the traditional site of Jesus' birth. The star that drew the wise men to see the baby Jesus is mirrored in the crypt of the church (FAR RIGHT) which reflects the devotion of centuries of pilgrims.

THE BOY JESUS

*After King Herod died, God told Joseph
that it was safe to return to Israel.
Since Herod's son was now king of Judaea,
Joseph took no chances.
He went back to Nazareth, in the northern
province of Galilee.
Jesus grew up in obscurity, until he was
twelve and approaching full adult
membership of the Jewish community . . .*

Every year the parents of Jesus went to Jerusalem for the Passover Festival. When Jesus was twelve years old, they went to the festival as usual.

When the festival was over, they started back home, but the boy Jesus stayed in Jerusalem. His parents did not know this; they thought that he was with the group, so they travelled a whole day and then started looking for him among their relatives and friends. They did not find him, so they went back to Jerusalem looking for him.

On the third day they found him in the Temple, sitting with the Jewish teachers listening to them and asking questions. All who heard him were amazed at his intelligent answers.

His parents were astonished when they saw him, and his mother said to him, 'My son, why have you done this to us? Your father and I have been terribly worried trying to find you.'

He answered them, 'Why did you have to look for me? Didn't you know that I had to be in my Father's house?'

But they did not understand his answer.

So Jesus went back with them to Nazareth, where he was obedient to them. His mother treasured all these things in her heart. Jesus grew both in body and in wisdom, gaining favour with God and men.

Luke 2

A family walks in present-day Nazareth (LEFT) where Jesus was brought up. At the age of twelve he was so engrossed in discussions in the temple area of Jerusalem (today the courtyard of the mosque, RIGHT) that his parents left without him.

A Voice in the Desert

When God sent his angel to tell Mary
she was to be the mother of Jesus,
he told her that her relative Elizabeth
was also expecting a baby.
That baby's name was John.
He was to be the last of the prophets,
with the special task of preparing God's
people for the coming of Jesus,
the promised Messiah.
When John was born,
his father Zechariah
was filled with the Holy Spirit . . .

Zechariah's prophecy
The Benedictus·

Blessed be the Lord God of Israel;
for he hath visited and redeemed
his people,
And hath raised up a horn of salvation
for us in the house of his servant David;
As he spake by the mouth
of his holy prophets,
which have been since the world began:
That we should be saved from our
enemies,
and from the hand of all that hate us . . .
And thou, child, shall be called
the prophet of the Highest:
for thou shalt go before the face
of the Lord to prepare his ways;
To give knowledge of salvation
unto his people
by the remission of their sins,
Through the tender mercy of our God;
whereby the dayspring from on high
hath visited us,
To give light to them that sit in darkness
and in the shadow of death,
to guide our feet into the way of peace.

Luke 1

It was the fifteenth year of the rule of the Emperor Tiberius; Pontius Pilate was governor of Judaea, Herod was ruler of Galilee . . . At that time the word of God came to John son of Zechariah in the desert.

So John went throughout the whole territory of the River Jordan, preaching, 'Turn away from your sins and be baptized, and God will forgive your sins.'

As it is written in the book of the prophet Isaiah:

'Someone is shouting in the desert:
''Get the road ready for the Lord;
make a straight path for him to travel!
Every valley must be filled up,
every hill and mountain levelled off.
The winding roads must be made straight,
and the rough paths made smooth.
All mankind will see God's salvation!'' '

Crowds of people came out to John to be baptized by him . . .

In many different ways John preached the Good News to the people and urged them to change their ways . . .

At that time Jesus arrived from Galilee and came to John at the Jordan to be baptized by him. But John tried to make him change his mind.

'I ought to be baptized by you,' John said, 'and yet you have come to me!'

But Jesus answered him, 'Let it be so for now. For in this way we shall do all that God requires.'

So John agreed.

As soon as Jesus was baptized, he came up out of the water. Then heaven was opened to him, and he saw the Spirit of God coming down like a dove and alighting on him. Then a voice said from heaven,

'This is my own dear Son, with whom I am pleased.'

Luke 3; Matthew 3

In the desert of Judea John the baptizer called men and women to turn away from their sin.

'IF YOU ARE GOD'S SON...'

Jesus returned from the Jordan full of the Holy Spirit and was led by the Spirit into the desert, where he was tempted by the Devil for forty days. In all that time he ate nothing, so that he was hungry when it was over.

The Devil said to him, 'If you are God's Son, order this stone to turn into bread.'

But Jesus answered, 'The scripture says, "Man cannot live on bread alone." '

Then the Devil took him up and showed him in a second all the kingdoms of the world.

'I will give you all this power and all this wealth,' the Devil told him. 'It has all been handed over to me, and I can give it to anyone I choose. All this will be yours, then, if you worship me.'

Jesus answered, 'The scripture says, "Worship the Lord your God and serve only him!" ' Then the Devil took him to Jerusalem and set him on the highest point of the Temple, and said to him, 'If you are God's Son, throw yourself down from here. For the scripture says, "God will order his angels to take good care of you." It also says, "They will hold you up with their hands so that not even your feet will be hurt on the stones." '

But Jesus answered, 'The scripture says, "Do not put the Lord your God to the test." '

When the Devil finished tempting Jesus in every way, he left him for a while.

Luke 4

In the rocky desert, Jesus faced up to the
temptations his ministry was to bring.

MANIFESTO

Jesus went to Galilee and preached the Good News from God.

'The right time has come,' he said, 'and the Kingdom of God is near! Turn away from your sins and believe the Good News!'

Mark 1

The declaration

And he came to Nazareth, where he had been brought up: and, as his custom was, he went into the synagogue on the sabbath day, and stood up for to read.

And there was delivered unto him the book of the prophet Esaias (Isaiah). And when he had opened the book, he found the place where it was written,

The Spirit of the Lord is upon me, because he hath anointed me to preach the gospel to the poor; he hath sent me to heal the brokenhearted, to preach deliverance to the captives, and recovering of sight to the blind, to set at liberty them that are bruised, To preach the acceptable year of the Lord.

And he closed the book, and he gave it again to the minister, and sat down. And the eyes of all them that were in the synagogue were fastened upon him.

And he began to say unto them, This day is this scripture fulfilled in your ears.

Luke 4

'COME WITH ME!'

Very early in his work Jesus began to
choose certain of his followers for
a special purpose.
They were ordinary people,
among them four fishermen . . .

As Jesus walked along the shore of Lake Galilee, he saw two brothers who were fishermen, Simon (called Peter) and his brother Andrew, catching fish in the lake with a net.

Jesus said to them, 'Come with me, and I will teach you to catch men.'

At once they left their nets and went with him.

He went on and saw two other brothers, James and John, the sons of Zebedee. They were in their boat with their father Zebedee, getting their nets ready. Jesus called them, and at once they left the boat and their father, and went with him.

Matthew 4

The Beatitudes

When Jesus spoke to those who followed him - people who were poor, without position or influence - he turned upside down all the accepted ideas of what makes for happiness. Is it the rich, the powerful, the successful, who are happy? No, said Jesus . . .

Blessed are the poor in spirit:
for theirs is the kingdom of heaven.
Blessed are they that mourn:
for they shall be comforted.
Blessed are the meek:
for they shall inherit the earth.
Blessed are they which do hunger
and thirst after righteousness:
for they shall be filled.
Blessed are the merciful:
for they shall obtain mercy.
Blessed are the pure in heart:
for they shall see God.
Blessed are the peacemakers:
for they shall be called
the children of God.
Blessed are they which are persecuted
for righteousness' sake: for theirs
is the kingdom of heaven.
Blessed are ye, when men shall revile you,
and persecute you, and shall say
all manner of evil against you falsely,
for my sake.
Rejoice, and be exceeding glad:
for great is your reward in heaven:
for so persecuted they the prophets
which were before you.
Matthew 5

Still today fishermen put out in small boats on Lake Galilee.

THE SERMON ON THE MOUNT

*Matthew, in his Gospel, provides
a collection of the teaching
and sayings of Jesus, known as
the Sermon on the Mount.*

Jesus' disciples
You are like salt for all mankind . . .
You are like light for the whole world. A city
built on a hill cannot be hidden. No one lights
a lamp and puts it under a bowl; instead he
puts it on the lampstand, where it gives light
for everyone in the house. In the same way
your light must shine before people, so that
they will see the good things you do and
praise your Father in heaven.

The narrow gate

Enter ye in at the strait gate:
for wide is the gate,
and broad is the way,
that leadeth to destruction,
and many there be which go in thereat:
because strait is the gate,
and narrow is the way,
which leadeth unto life,
and few there be that find it.
Matthew 7

The Law
Do not think that I have come to do away
with the Law of Moses and the teachings of
the prophets. I have not come to do away
with them, but to make their teachings come
true.

Wrong-thinking and wrong-doing
It was said . . . Do not commit murder . . .
Do not commit adultery. But now I tell you:
anyone who looks at a woman and wants to
possess her is guilty of committing adultery
with her in his heart.

Giving
When you give something to a needy person,
do not make a big show of it . . . do it in such a
way that even your closest friend will not
know about it. Then it will be a private
matter. And your Father, who sees what you
do in private, will reward you.

Treasure in heaven
Do not store up riches for yourselves here on
earth, where moths and rust destroy, and
robbers break in and steal. Instead, store up
riches for yourselves in heaven, where moths
and rust cannot destroy, and robbers cannot
break in and steal. For your heart will always
be where your riches are.

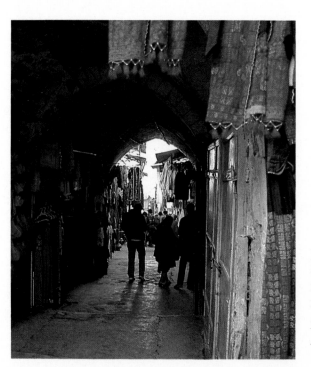

Priorities

No one can be a slave of two masters; he will hate one and love the other; he will be loyal to one and despise the other. You cannot serve both God and money.

This is why I tell you not to be worried about the food and drink you need in order to stay alive, or about clothes for your body. After all, isn't life worth more than food? And isn't the body worth more than clothes? Look at the birds flying around: they do not sow seeds, gather a harvest and put it in barns; yet your Father in heaven takes care of them! Aren't you worth much more than birds? Can any of you live a bit longer by worrying about it?

And why worry about clothes? Look how the wild flowers grow: they do not work or make clothes for themselves. But I tell you that not even King Solomon with all his wealth had clothes as beautiful as one of these flowers. It is God who clothes the wild grass – grass that is here today and gone tomorrow, burnt up in the oven. Won't he be all the more sure to clothe you? How little faith you have!

So do not start worrying: 'Where will my food come from? or my drink? or my clothes? (These are the things the pagans are always concerned about.) Your Father in heaven knows that you need all these things. Instead, be concerned above everything else with the Kingdom of God and with what he requires of you, and he will provide you with all these other things. So do not worry about tomorrow; it will have enough worries of its own. There is no need to add to the troubles each day brings.

Judging others

Do not judge others, so that God will not judge you, for God will judge you in the same way as you judge others, and he will apply to you the same rules you apply to others. Why, then, do you look at the speck in your brother's eye, and pay no attention to the log in your own eye? How dare you say to your brother, 'Please, let me take that speck out of your eye,' when you have a log in your own eye? You hypocrite! First take the log out of your own eye, and then you will be able to see clearly to take the speck out of your brother's eye.

Matthew 5–7

The golden rule

**Therefore all things whatsoever ye would that men should do to you,
do ye even so to them:
for this is the law and the prophets.**
Matthew 7

The teaching of Jesus was radical and new. But it was practical and relevant to ordinary people.

'TEACH US TO PRAY'

Throughout the hours of daylight Jesus was surrounded by people. Yet he always made time – and found quiet – to pray. Seeing this, his disciples asked him to teach them how to pray.

When you pray, go to your room, close the door, and pray to your Father, who is unseen. And your Father, who sees what you do in private, will reward you.

When you pray, do not use a lot of meaningless words, as the pagans do, who think that God will hear them because their prayers are long. Do not be like them. Your Father already knows what you need before you ask him. This, then, is how you should pray:

The Lord's Prayer

Our Father which art in heaven,
Hallowed be thy name.
Thy kingdom come.
Thy will be done in earth,
as it is in heaven.
Give us this day our daily bread.
And forgive us our debts,
as we forgive our debtors.
And lead us not into temptation,
but deliver us from evil:
For thine is the kingdom, and the power,
and the glory, for ever. Amen
Matthew 6

Ask, and you will receive; seek, and you will find; knock, and the door will be opened to you. For everyone who asks will receive, and anyone who seeks will find, and the door will be opened to him who knocks.

Would any of you who are fathers give your son a stone when he asks for bread? Or would you give him a snake when he asks for a fish? Bad as you are, you know how to give good things to your children. How much more, then, will your Father in heaven give good things to those who ask him!
Matthew 7

And I tell you more: whenever two of you on earth agree about anything you pray for, it will be done for you by my Father in heaven. For where two or three come together in my name, I am there with them.
Matthew 18

Jesus would withdraw to the hills overlooking Lake Galilee to pray; often before dawn he prayed for the busy day that lay ahead.

29

A Life of Love

Jesus' own life – and death – is a demonstration of God's love in action: self-giving, self-sacrificing love to the uttermost. He also calls his followers to a life of love, through the transforming power of his Spirit within them. One day he was asked which is the greatest of God's commandments . . .

Jesus answered, ' "Love the Lord your God with all your heart, with all your soul, and with all your mind." This is the greatest and the most important commandment. The second most important commandment is like it: "Love your neighbour as you love yourself." The whole Law of Moses and the teaching of the prophets depend on these two commandments.'
Matthew 22

My commandment is this: love one another, just as I love you. The greatest love a person can have for his friends is to give his life for them.
John 15

Love your enemies, do good to those who hate you, bless those who curse you, and pray for those who ill-treat you. If anyone hits you on one cheek, let him hit the other one too; if someone takes your coat, let him have your shirt as well. Give to everyone who asks you for something, and when someone takes what is yours, do not ask for it back. Do for others just what you want them to do for you.

If you love only the people who love you, why should you receive a blessing? Even sinners love those who love them! And if you do good only to those who do good to you, why should you receive a blessing? Even sinners do that! . . . No! Love your enemies and do good to them; lend and expect nothing back . . . Be merciful just as your Father is merciful.
Luke 6

Love in action
'The Good Samaritan'

In answer to the question, 'Who is my neighbour?' Jesus told this story about one of the despised Samaritans, people whom the Jews looked on as inferior:

'There was once a man who was going down from Jerusalem to Jericho when robbers attacked him, stripped him, and beat him up, leaving him half dead.

'It so happened that a priest was going down that road; but when he saw the man, he walked on by, on the other side. In the same way a Levite also came along, went over and looked at the man, and then walked on by, on the other side.

'But a Samaritan who was travelling that way came upon the man, and when he saw him, his heart was filled with pity. He went over to him, poured oil and wine on his wounds and bandaged them; then he put the man on his own animal and took him to an inn, where he took care of him. The next day he took out two silver coins and gave them to the innkeeper.

' "Take care of him," he told the innkeeper," and when I come back this way, I will pay you whatever else you spend on him." '

And Jesus concluded, 'In your opinion, which one of these three acted like a neighbour towards the man attacked by the robbers?'

The teacher of the Law answered, 'The one who was kind to him.'

Jesus replied, 'You go, then, and do the same.'

Luke 10

The road from Jerusalem to Jericho, scene of Jesus' story of the Good Samaritan, goes steeply down through a rocky desert area. It would have been easy for his hearers to picture the story of a man who was robbed and beaten up.

THE KINGDOM OF HEAVEN

Jesus often used 'parables' in his teaching. These stories-with-a-point use everyday examples of life to get their message across. But they were more than simple illustrations. 'The reason I use parables in talking to them,' Jesus said, 'is that they look, but do not see, and they listen, but do not understand.' People have 'stopped up their ears' and closed their eyes to God's message. Only those who really want to know and to follow Jesus will find out the meaning of his parables. Jesus was appealing, not to idle curiosity, but to the wills of those who heard him.

The yeast

The Kingdom of heaven is like this. A woman takes some yeast and mixes it with forty litres of flour until the whole batch of dough rises.

The Parable of the Sower

Behold, a sower went forth to sow;
And when he sowed,
some seeds fell by the way side,
and the fowls came and devoured
them up:
Some fell upon stony places,
where they had not much earth:
and forthwith they sprung up,
because they had no deepness of earth:
And when the sun was up, they were
scorched; and because they had no root,
they withered away.
And some fell among thorns;
and the thorns sprung up,
and choked them:
But other fell into good ground,
and brought forth fruit,
some an hundredfold, some sixtyfold,
some thirtyfold.
Who hath ears to hear, let him hear . . .

Hear ye therefore the parable of the sower.
When any one heareth the word
of the kingdom, and understandeth it not,
then cometh the wicked one, and catcheth
away that which was sown in his heart.
This is he which received seed
by the way side.
But he that received the seed into stony
places, the same is he that
heareth the word,
and anon with joy receiveth it;
Yet hath he not root in himself,
but dureth for a while:
for when tribulation or persecution
ariseth because of the word,
by and by he is offended.
He also that received seed among the
thorns is he that heareth the word;
and the care of this world,
and the deceitfulness of riches,
choke the word,
and he becometh unfruitful.
But he that received seed into the good
ground is he that heareth the word,
and understandeth it; which also
beareth fruit, and bringeth forth,
some an hundredfold, some sixty,
some thirty.

Matthew 13

Hidden treasure

The Kingdom of heaven is like this. A man happens to find a treasure hidden in a field. He covers it up again, and is so happy that he goes and sells everything he has and then goes back and buys that field.

The pearl

The Kingdom of heaven is like this. A man is looking for fine pearls, and when he finds one that is unusually fine, he goes and sells everything he has, and buys that pearl.

Matthew 13

The mustard seed

The Kingdom of heaven is like this. A man takes a mustard seed and sows it in his field. It is the smallest of all seeds, but when it grows up, it is the biggest of all plants. It becomes a tree, so that birds come and make their nests in its branches.

Jesus used the vivid imagery of the market-place and ordinary farming and working life to confront his hearers with his message.

'YOU MUST BE BORN AGAIN'

Jesus came not only to announce God's Kingdom and tell people about it, he came to invite them in – not as aliens, but as sons and daughters of God.
This is how he explained it to one enquirer . . .

There was a Jewish leader named Nicodemus, who belonged to the party of the Pharisees. One night he went to Jesus and said to him, 'Rabbi, we know that you are a teacher sent by God. No one could perform the miracles you are doing unless God were with him.'

Jesus answered, 'I am telling you the truth: no one can see the Kingdom of God unless he is born again.'

'How can a grown man be born again?' Nicodemus asked. 'He certainly cannot enter his mother's womb and be born a second time!'

'I am telling you the truth,' replied Jesus. 'No one can enter the Kingdom of God unless he is born of water and the Spirit. A person is born physically of human parents, but he is born spiritually of the Spirit. Do not be surprised because I tell you that you must all be born again. The wind blows wherever it wishes; you hear the sound it makes, but you do not know where it comes from or where it is going. It is like that with everyone who is born of the Spirit . . .

' . . the Son of Man must be lifted up, so that everyone who believes in him may have eternal life. For God loved the world so much that he gave his only Son, so that everyone who believes in him may not die but have eternal life. For God did not send his Son into the world to be its judge, but to be its saviour.'

John 3

Can people really become like little children? Can they be reborn, and escape the inborn disease of sin and death?

Jesus and the children

Then were there brought unto him little children, that he should put his hands on them, and pray: and the disciples rebuked them.
But Jesus said, Suffer little children, and forbid them not, to come unto me: for of such is the kingdom of heaven. And he laid his hands on them.
Matthew 19

Verily I say unto you, except ye be converted, and become as little children, ye shall not enter into the kingdom of heaven.
Matthew 18

FORGIVEN AND FORGIVING

Jesus came to make God's forgiveness available to all who turned to him, genuinely sorry for their wrongdoing and wanting a fresh start.
But those whom God freely forgives are expected in their turn to be forgiving.

Peter came to Jesus and asked, 'Lord, if my brother keeps on sinning against me, how many times do I have to forgive him? Seven times?'

'No, not seven times,' answered Jesus, 'but seventy times seven.'

Matthew 18

Authority to forgive

Jesus . . . said to the paralysed man, 'Courage, my son! Your sins are forgiven.'

Then some teachers of the Law said to themselves, 'This man is speaking blasphemy!'

Jesus perceived what they were thinking, so he said, 'Why are you thinking such evil things? Is it easier to say, "Your sins are forgiven," or to say, "Get up and walk"? I will prove to you, then, that the Son of Man has authority on earth to forgive sins.' So he said to the paralysed man, 'Get up, pick up your bed, and go home!'

The man got up and went home. When the people saw it, they were afraid, and praised God for giving such authority to men.

Matthew 9

The teaching of Jesus was geared to the needs and relationships of people in their everyday lives.

The man who owed millions

'Once there was a king who decided to check on his servants' accounts. He had just begun to do so when one of them was brought in who owed him millions of pounds. The servant did not have enough to pay his debt, so the king ordered him to be sold as a slave, with his wife and his children and all that he had, in order to pay the debt. The servant fell on his knees before the king.

' "Be patient with me," he begged, "and I will pay you everything!"

'The king felt sorry for him, so he forgave him the debt and let him go.

'Then the man went out and met one of his fellow-servants who owed him a few pounds. He grabbed him and started choking him.

' "Pay back what you owe me!" he said.

'His fellow-servant fell down and begged him, "Be patient with me, and I will pay you back!"

'But he refused; instead, he had him thrown into jail until he should pay the debt. When the other servants saw what had happened, they were very upset and went to the king and told him everything. So he called the servant in.

' "You worthless slave!" he said. "I forgave you the whole amount you owed me, just because you asked me to. You should have had mercy on your fellow-servant, just as I had mercy on you." The king was very angry, and he sent the servant to jail to be punished until he should pay back the whole amount." '

And Jesus concluded, 'That is how my Father in heaven will treat every one of you unless you forgive your brother from your heart.'

Matthew 18

THE INVITATION

Come unto me,
all ye that labour and are heavy laden,
and I will give you rest.
Take my yoke upon you, and learn of me;
for I am meek and lowly in heart:
and ye shall find rest unto your souls.
For my yoke is easy,
and my burden is light.

Matthew 11

Zacchaeus

Jesus went on into Jericho and was passing through.

There was à chief tax collector there named Zacchaeus, who was rich. He was trying to see who Jesus was, but he was a little man and could not see Jesus because of the crowd. So he ran ahead of the crowd and climbed a sycomore tree to see Jesus, who was going to pass that way.

When Jesus came to that place, he looked up and said to Zacchaeus, 'Hurry down, Zacchaeus; because I must stay in your house today.'

Zacchaeus hurried down and welcomed him with great joy. All the people who saw it started grumbling, 'This man has gone as a guest to the home of a sinner!'

Zacchaeus stood up and said to the Lord, 'Listen, sir! I will give half my belongings to the poor, and if I have cheated anyone, I will pay him back four times as much.'

Jesus said to him, 'Salvation has come to this house today, for this man, also, is a descendant of Abraham. The Son of Man came to seek and to save the lost.'
Luke 19

The Parable of the Great Feast

Jesus said . . . 'There was once a man who was giving a great feast to which he invited many people.

When it was time for the feast, he sent his servant to tell his guests, "Come, everything is ready!"

'But they all began, one after another, to make excuses.

'The first one told the servant, "I have bought a field and must go and look at it; please accept my apologies."

'Another one said, "I have bought five pairs of oxen and am on my way to try them out; please accept my apologies."

'Another one said, "I have just got married, and for that reason I cannot come."

'The servant went back and told all this to his master. The master was furious and said to his servant, "Hurry out to the streets and alleys of the town, and bring back the poor, the crippled, the blind, and the lame."

'Soon the servant said, "Your order has been carried out, sir, but there is room for more."

'So the master said to the servant, "Go out to the country roads and lanes and make people come in, so that my house will be full. I tell you all that none of those men who were invited will taste my dinner!" '
Luke 14

'Come unto me,' Jesus said to those who 'labour and are heavy-laden'; to people like Zacchaeus, from the town of Jericho which is pictured here.

FOOD FOR THE HUNGRY

'There were so many people coming and going that Jesus and his disciples didn't even have time to eat.'
They simply had to get away somewhere quiet to rest. So they rowed across Lake Galilee. But people saw them leave and ran round the shore to be there before the boat landed. Jesus' heart went out to them, and the rest-day became a day of teaching . . .

His disciples came to him and said, 'It is already very late, and this is a lonely place. Send the people away, and let them go to the nearby farms and villages in order to buy themselves something to eat.'

'You yourselves give them something to eat,' Jesus answered.

They asked, 'Do you want us to go and spend two hundred silver coins on bread in order to feed them?'

So Jesus asked them, 'How much bread have you got? Go and see.'

When they found out, they told him, 'Five loaves and also two fish.'

Jesus then told his disciples to make all the people divide into groups and sit down on the green grass. So the people sat down in rows, in groups of a hundred and groups of fifty. Then Jesus took the five loaves and the two fish, looked up to heaven, and gave thanks to God. He broke the loaves and gave them to

his disciples to distribute to the people. He also divided the fish among them all. Everyone ate and had enough.

Then the disciples took up twelve baskets full of what was left of the bread and the fish. The number of the men who were fed was five thousand.

Mark 6

My Father giveth you the true
bread from heaven.
For the bread of God is he which cometh
down from heaven, and giveth life
unto the world. Then said they unto him,
Lord, evermore give us this bread.
And Jesus said unto them,
I am the bread of life:
he that cometh to me shall never hunger;
and he that believeth on me
shall never thirst.

John 6

Mount Hermon rises behind the hills of Galilee which slope down to the lake, scene of the miracles and teaching of Jesus.

'FOLLOW ME'

*Jesus attracted a great following.
Many came to him for healing.
Some came eager to listen to what he had
ɔ say. But a crowd draws a crowd and some
were merely curious to see him,
or hoping for a miracle.
When Jesus began to point out the cost
of following him, many went away.*

Trouble to come

I tell you my friends, do not be afraid of those who kill the body but cannot afterwards do anything worse. I will show you whom to fear: fear God, who after killing, has the authority to throw into hell. Believe me, he is the one you must fear!

Aren't five sparrows sold for two pennies?

Yet not one sparrow is forgotten by God. Even the hairs of your head have all been counted. So do not be afraid; you are worth much more than many sparrows!
Luke 12

The cost . . .

Whoever comes to me cannot be my disciple unless he loves me more than he loves his father and his mother, his wife and his children, his brothers and his sisters, and himself as well. Whoever does not carry his own cross and come after me cannot be my disciple.

If one of you is planning to build a tower, he sits down first and works out what it will cost, to see if he has enough money to finish the job.
Luke 14

If anyone wants to come with me . . . he must forget self, carry his cross, and follow me. For whoever wants to save his own life will lose it; but whoever loses his life for me and for the gospel will save it. Does a person gain anything if he wins the whole world but loses his life? Of course not! There is nothing he can give to regain his life.
Mark 8

. . . and the reward

Peter spoke up.

'Look,' he said, 'we have left everything and followed you. What will we have?'

Jesus said to them, 'You can be sure that when the Son of Man sits on his glorious throne in the New Age, then you twelve followers of mine will also sit on thrones, to rule the twelve tribes of Israel. And everyone who has left houses or brothers or sisters or father or mother or children or fields for my sake, will receive a hundred times more and will be given eternal life. But many who now are first will be last, and many who now are last will be first.

Matthew 19

Least and greatest

The rulers of the heathen have power over them, and the leaders have complete authority. This, however, is not how it shall be among you. If one of you wants to be great, he must be the servant of the rest; and if one of you wants to be first, he must be your slave – like the Son of Man, who did not come to be served, but to serve and to give his life to redeem many people.

Matthew 20

A man said to Jesus, 'I will follow you wherever you go.'

Jesus said to him, 'Foxes have holes, and birds have nests, but the Son of Man has nowhere to lie down and rest.'

He said to another man, 'Follow me.'

But that man said, 'Sir, first let me go back and bury my father.'

Jesus answered, 'Let the dead bury their own dead. You go and proclaim the Kingdom of God.'

Another man said, 'I will follow you, sir; but first let me go and say good-bye to my family.'

Jesus said to him, 'Anyone who starts to plough and then keeps looking back is of no use to the Kingdom of God.'

Luke 9

FREEDOM!

*Jesus came to proclaim liberty,
to set us free. When he healed,
he set people free not simply from the
pain and limitation of illness, but
from a far more serious and far-reaching
'bondage' – the implacable hold of sin.
This freedom he offered to all,
sick or well.*

Free men and slaves

Jesus said to those who believed in him, 'If you obey my teaching, you are really my disciples; you will know the truth, and the truth will set you free.'

'We are the descendants of Abraham,' they answered, 'and we have never been anybody's slaves. What do you mean, then, by saying, "You will be free"?'

Jesus said to them, 'I am telling you the truth: everyone who sins is a slave of sin. A slave does not belong to a family permanently, but a son belongs there for ever. If the Son sets you free, then you will be really free.'

John 8

Behind the birds flying free over Lake Galilee rise the distant hills where Jesus healed the man who was possessed.

An extreme case

Jesus and his disciples sailed on over to the territory of Gerasa, which is across the lake from Galilee. As Jesus stepped ashore, he was met by a man from the town who had demons in him. For a long time this man had gone without clothes and would not stay at home, but spent his time in the burial caves. When he saw Jesus, he gave a loud cry, threw himself down at his feet, and shouted, 'Jesus, Son of the Most High God! What do you want with me? I beg you, don't punish me!'

He said this because Jesus had ordered the evil spirit to go out of him. Many times it had siezed him, and even though he was kept a prisoner, his hands and feet fastened with chains, he would break the chains and be driven by the demon out into the desert.

Jesus asked him, 'What is your name?'

'My name is "Mob",' he answered - because many demons had gone into him. The demons begged Jesus not to send them into the abyss.

There was a large herd of pigs near by, feeding on the hillside. So the demons begged Jesus to let them go into the pigs, and he let them. They went out of the man and into the pigs. The whole herd rushed down the side of the cliff into the lake and was drowned.

The men who had been taking care of the pigs saw what happened, so they ran off and spread the news in the town and among the farms. People went out to see what had happened, and when they came to Jesus, they found the man from whom the demons had gone out sitting at the feet of Jesus, clothed and in his right mind; and they were all afraid.

Luke 8

The crippled woman

One Sabbath Jesus was teaching in a synagogue. A woman there had an evil spirit that had made her ill for eighteen years; she was bent over and could not straighten up at all.

When Jesus saw her, he called out to her, 'Woman, you are free from your illness!' He placed his hands on her, and at once she straightened herself up and praised God.

Luke 13

THE CHOSEN TWELVE

Jesus . . . called to himself the men he wanted. They came to him, and he chose twelve, whom he named apostles.

'I have chosen you to be with me,' he told them. 'I will also send you out to preach, and you will have authority to drive out demons.'

These are the twelve he chose: Simon (Jesus gave him the name Peter); James and his brother John, the sons of Zebedee (Jesus gave them the name Boanerges, which means 'Men of Thunder'); Andrew, Philip, Bartholomew, Matthew, Thomas, James son of Alphaeus, Thaddaeus, Simon the Patriot, and Judas Iscariot, who betrayed Jesus.

Mark 3

Matthew, the tax collector

As Jesus walked along, he saw a tax collector, named Matthew, sitting in his office. He said to him, 'Follow me.'

Matthew got up and followed him.

While Jesus was having a meal in Matthew's house, many tax collectors and other outcasts came and joined Jesus and his disciples at the table.

Some Pharisees saw this and asked his disciples, 'Why does your teacher eat with such people?'

Jesus heard them and answered, 'People who are well do not need a doctor, but only those who are sick . . . I have not come to call respectable people, but outcasts.'

Matthew 9

Several of the closest followers of Jesus were fishermen on Lake Galilee.

'WHO ARE YOU?'

John the Baptist, meantime, was in trouble.
His outspokenness telling King Herod
that it was wrong to have married
his brother's wife resulted in prison.
But even there news reached John
of what Jesus was doing.
Was Jesus the promised Messiah?

When John the Baptist heard in prison about the things that Christ was doing, he sent some of his disciples to him.

'Tell us,' they asked Jesus, 'are you the one John said was going to come, or should we expect someone else?'

Jesus answered, 'Go back and tell John what you are hearing and seeing: the blind can see, the lame can walk, those who suffer from dreaded skin-diseases are made clean, the deaf hear, the dead are brought back to

life, and the Good News is preached to the poor. How happy are those who have no doubts about me!'
Matthew 11

The gospel preached to the poor (LEFT) was evidence to John the Baptist that Jesus really was the promised Messiah. Sheep grazing on the hillsides above Lake Galilee are a reminder of the lambs sacrificed for sin in the Old Testament.

'The Lamb of God' John's tribute to Jesus

Behold the Lamb of God, which taketh away the sin of the world.
This is he of whom I said, After me cometh a man which is preferred before me: for he was before me.
John 1

Ye yourselves bear me witness, that I said, I am not the Christ, but that I am sent before him.
He that hath the bride is the bridegroom: but the friend of the bridegroom, which standeth and heareth him, rejoiceth greatly because of the bridegroom's voice: this my joy therefore is fulfilled.
He must increase, but I must decrease.
John 3

'THIS IS MY SON'

John was beheaded, and the news was brought to Jesus. Some time later, Jesus and his disciples travelled to the far north of Israel.

Jesus went to the territory near the town of Caesarea Philippi, where he asked his disciples, 'Who do people say the Son of Man is?'

'Some say John the Baptist,' they answered. 'Others say Elijah, while others say Jeremiah or some other prophet.'

'What about you?' he asked them. 'Who do you say I am?'

Simon Peter answered, 'You are the Messiah, the Son of the living God.' . . .

From that time on Jesus began to say plainly to his disciples, 'I must go to Jerusalem and suffer much from the elders, the chief priests, and the teachers of the Law. I will be put to death, but three days later I will be raised to life . . .'

Six days later Jesus took with him Peter and the brothers James and John and led them up a high mountain where they were alone. As they looked on, a change came over Jesus: his face was shining like the sun, and his clothes were dazzling white. Then the three disciples saw Moses and Elijah talking with Jesus.

So Peter spoke up and said to Jesus, 'Lord, how good it is that we are here! If you wish, I will make three tents here, one for you, one for Moses, and one for Elijah.'

While he was talking, a shining cloud came over them, and a voice from the cloud said, 'This is my own dear Son, with whom I am pleased – listen to him!'

Matthew 16 and 17

Strikingly it was at Caesarea Philippi (RIGHT) that Peter made his confession of Jesus as 'Messiah, the Son of the living God'. Not only was the town dedicated to the Roman Caesar, it was also a centre for worship of the nature god Pan, and the source of the River Jordan, the springs of Israel's life and prosperity. Rising above the ancient town is Mount Hermon (LEFT), a natural site for the transfiguration of Jesus.

LIGHT FOR A DARK WORLD

I am the light of the world:
he that followeth me shall not walk
in darkness, but shall have the light of life.
John 8

In the dark
The light has come into the world, but people
love darkness rather than the light, because
their deeds are evil. Anyone who does evil
things hates the light and will not come to the
light, because he does not want his evil deeds
to be shown up. But whoever does what is
true comes to the light in order that the light
may show that what he did was in obedience
to God.
John 3

Light to Walk by
The light will be among you a little longer.
Continue on your way while you have the
light, so that the darkness will not come upon
you; for the one who walks in the dark does
not know where he is going. Believe in the
light, then, while you have it, so that you will
be the people of the light.
John 12

From darkness to light
Whoever believes in me believes not only in
me but also in him who sent me. Whoever
sees me sees also him who sent me. I have
come into the world as light, so that everyone
who believes in me should not remain in the
darkness.
John 12

The Pool of Siloam was the result of an ancient engineering feat, bringing water through a rock-hewn tunnel. Here the man born blind was given his sight and a new life.

The man born blind

As Jesus was walking along, he saw a man who had been born blind. His disciples asked him, 'Teacher, whose sin caused him to be born blind? Was it his own or his parents' sin?'

Jesus answered, 'His blindness has nothing to do with his sins or his parents' sins. He is blind so that God's power might be seen at work in him. As long as it is day, we must keep on doing the work of him who sent me; night is coming when no one can work. While I am in the world, I am the light for the world.'

After he said this, Jesus spat on the ground and made some mud with the spittle; he rubbed the mud on the man's eyes and said, 'Go and wash your face in the Pool of Siloam.' (This name means 'Sent'.) So the man went, washed his face, and came back seeing . . .

Jesus said, 'I came to this world to judge, so that the blind should see and those who see should become blind.'

Some Pharisees who were there with him heard him say this and asked him, 'Surely you don't mean that we are blind, too?'

Jesus answered, 'If you were blind, then you would not be guilty; but since you claim that you can see, this means that you are still guilty.'

John 9

FAITH THAT MOVES MOUNTAINS

*The wonders Jesus did during his life
on earth were intended to lead to faith –
belief in him – on the part of those
who saw them. He was constantly amazed
at people's unbelief – the stubborn refusal
of many to believe the evidence of their
own eyes. He required faith
from those who wanted to be healed –
or the friends who brought them to him.
It wasn't the amount of faith that
mattered, but its direction.
There was a boy possessed by an evil spirit
brought to Jesus. His disciples were
unable to heal him . . .*

Jesus said to them, 'How unbelieving you people are! How long must I stay with you? How long do I have to put up with you? Bring the boy to me!' They brought him to Jesus.

As soon as the spirit saw Jesus, it threw the boy into a fit, so that he fell on the ground and rolled round, foaming at the mouth.

'How long has he been like this?' Jesus asked the father.

'Ever since he was a child,' he replied. 'Many times the evil spirit has tried to kill him by throwing him in the fire and into water. Have pity on us and help us, if you possibly can!'

'Yes,' said Jesus, 'if you yourself can! Everything is possible for the person who has faith.'

The father at once cried out, 'I do have faith, but not enough. Help me to have more!'

Jesus noticed that the crowd was closing in on them, so he gave a command to the evil spirit.

'Deaf and dumb spirit,' he said, 'I order you to come out of the boy and never go into him again!'

Then the disciples came to Jesus in private and asked him, 'Why couldn't we drive the demon out?'

'It was because you haven't enough faith,' answered Jesus. 'I assure you that if you have faith as big as a mustard seed, you can say to this hill, "Go from here to there!" and it will go. You could do anything!'
Mark 9 and Matthew 17

The ancient synagogue at Capernaum, sponsored in the time of Jesus by a Roman centurion, shows signs even in these ruins dating from several centuries later of mixed Jewish and Roman design.

A Roman soldier's faith

When Jesus entered Capernaum, a Roman officer met him and begged for help:

'Sir, my servant is sick in bed at home, unable to move and suffering terribly.'

'I will go and make him well,' Jesus said. 'Oh no, sir,' answered the officer. 'I do not deserve to have you come into my house. Just give the order, and my servant will get well. I, too, am a man under the authority of superior officers, and I have soldiers under me. I order this one, "Go!" and he goes; and I order that one, "Come!" and he comes; and I order my slave, "Do this!" and he does it.'

When Jesus heard this, he was surprised and said to the people following him, 'I tell you, I have never found anyone in Israel with faith like this.'

Matthew 8

SHEPHERD OF THE SHEEP

Jesus went round visiting all the towns and villages. He taught in the synagogues, preached the Good News about the Kingdom, and healed people with every kind of disease and sickness.

As he saw the crowds, his heart was filled with pity for them, because they were worried and helpless, like sheep without a shepherd.

Matthew 9

Shepherds today still lead and care for their flocks. Jesus is like the good shepherd, ready to protect his sheep, willing even to die for them.

The good shepherd
The man who goes in through the gate is the shepherd of the sheep. The gatekeeper opens the gate for him; the sheep hear his voice as he calls his own sheep by name, and he leads them out. When he has brought them out, he goes ahead of them, and the sheep follow him, because they know his voice . . .

I am the good shepherd, who is willing to die for the sheep. When the hired man, who is not a shepherd, and does not own the sheep, sees a wolf coming, he leaves the sheep and runs away; so the wolf snatches the sheep and scatters them. The hired man runs away because he is only a hired man and does not care about the sheep.

I am the good shepherd. As the Father knows me and I know the Father, in the same way I know my sheep and they know me. And I am willing to die for them.

John 10

The lost sheep

Suppose one of you has a hundred sheep and loses one of them - what does he do? He leaves the other ninety-nine sheep in the pasture and goes looking for the one that got lost until he finds it. When he finds it, he is so happy that he puts it on his shoulders and carries it back home.

Then he calls all his friends and neighbours together and says to them, 'I am so happy I found my lost sheep. Let us celebrate!'

In the same way, I tell you, there will be more joy in heaven over one sinner who repents than over ninety-nine respectable people who do not need to repent.

Luke 15

THE GIFT OF LIFE

I am come that they might have life, and that they might have it more abundantly.
John 10

Whoever believes in the Son has eternal life; whoever disobeys the Son will not have life, but will remain under God's punishment.
John 3

What my Father wants is that all who see the Son and believe in him should have eternal life. And I will raise them to life on the last day.

I am telling you the truth: he who believes has eternal life.
John 6

You study the Scriptures, because you think that in them you will find eternal life. And these very Scriptures speak about me! Yet you are not willing to come to me in order to have life.
John 5

'What gives life is God's Spirit; man's power is of no use at all. The words I have spoken to you bring God's life-giving Spirit. Yet some of you do not believe . . . This is the very reason I told you that no one can come to me unless the Father makes it possible for him to do so.'

Because of this, many of Jesus' followers turned back and would not go with him any more. So he asked the twelve disciples, 'And you – would you also like to leave?'

Simon Peter answered him, 'Lord, to whom would we go? You have the words that give eternal life. And now we believe and know that you are the Holy One who has come from God.'
John 6

'You study the Scriptures,' said Jesus, 'and they speak about me!' Real life is to be found in him alone. Just as he met the woman at the well, so he meets us at our point of need and gives us new life.

The rich man

A Jewish leader asked Jesus, 'Good Teacher, what must I do to receive eternal life?'

'Why do you call me good?' Jesus asked him. 'No one is good except God alone. You know the commandments: 'Do not commit adultery; do not commit murder; do not steal; do not accuse anyone falsely; respect your father and your mother." '

The man replied, 'Ever since I was young, I have obeyed all these commandments.'

When Jesus heard this, he said to him, 'There is still one more thing you need to do. Sell all you have and give the money to the poor, and you will have riches in heaven; then come and follow me.'

But when the man heard this, he became very sad, because he was very rich.

Jesus saw that he was sad and said, 'How hard it is for rich people to enter the Kingdom of God! It is much harder for a rich person to enter the Kingdom of God than for a camel to go through the eye of a needle.'

The people who heard him asked, 'Who, then, can be saved?'

Jesus answered, 'What is impossible for man is possible for God.'

Luke 18

The woman at the well

In Samaria he came to a town named Sychar, which was not far from the field that Jacob had given to his son Joseph. Jacob's well was there, and Jesus, tired out by the journey, sat down by the well. It was about noon.

A Samaritan woman came to draw some water, and Jesus said to her, 'Give me a drink of water.' (His disciples had gone into town to buy food.)

The woman answered, 'You are a Jew, and I am a Samaritan - so how can you ask me for a drink?' (Jews will not use the same cups and bowls that Samaritans use.)

Jesus answered, 'If only you knew what God gives and who it is that is asking you for a drink, you would ask him, and he would give you life-giving water.'

'Sir,' the woman said, 'you haven't got a bucket, and the well is deep. Where would you get that life-giving water? It was our ancestor Jacob who gave us this well; he and his sons and his flocks all drank from it. You don't claim to be greater than Joseph, do you?'

Jesus answered, 'Whoever drinks this water will be thirsty again, but whoever drinks the water that I will give him will never be thirsty again. The water that I will give him will become in him a spring which will provide him with life-giving water and give him eternal life.'

'Sir,' the woman said, 'give me that water!'

John 4

JEALOUSY

*One day when tax collectors and
other outcasts came to listen to Jesus,
the Pharisees and the Teachers of the Law
started grumbling, "This man welcomes
outcasts and even eats with them!"
So Jesus told them this parable . . .'*

Parable of the Prodigal Son

A certain man had two sons:
And the younger of them said to his father,
Father, give me the portion of goods
that falleth to me.
And he divided unto them his living.
And not many days after
the younger son gathered all together,
and took his journey into a far country,
and there wasted his substance
with riotous living.
And when he had spent all,
there arose a mighty famine in that land;
and he began to be in want.
And he went and joined himself
to a citizen of that country;
and he sent him into his fields
to feed swine.
And he would fain have filled his belly
with the husks that the swine did eat:
and no man gave unto him.
And when he came to himself, he said,
How many hired servants of my father's
have bread enough and to spare,
and I perish with hunger!
I will arise and go to my father,
and will say unto him,
Father, I have sinned against heaven,
and before thee,
And am no more worthy to be called
thy son:
make me as one of thy hired servants.
And he arose, and came to his father.
But when he was yet a great way off,
his father saw him, and had compassion,
and ran, and fell on his neck,
and kissed him.
And the son said unto him, Father, I have
sinned against heaven, and in thy sight,
and am no more worthy
to be called thy son.
But the father said to his servants,
Bring forth the best robe, and put it
on him; and put a ring on his hand,
and shoes on his feet:
And bring hither the fatted calf,
and kill it; and let us eat,
and be merry:
For this my son was dead, and is alive
again; he was lost, and is found.
And they began to be merry.
Now his elder son was in the field:
and as he came and drew nigh
to the house,
he heard musick and dancing.
And he called one of the servants,
and asked what these things meant.
And he said unto him,
Thy brother is come;
and thy father hath killed the fatted
calf, because he hath received him
safe and sound.
And he was angry, and would not go in:
therefore came his father out,
and intreated him.
And he answering said to his father,
Lo, these many years do I serve thee,
neither transgressed I at any time
thy commandment:
and yet thou never gavest
me a kid, that I might make merry
with my friends:
But as soon as this thy son was come,
which hath devoured thy living
with harlots,
thou hast killed for him the fatted calf.
And he said unto him,
Son, thou art ever with me,
and all that I have is thine.
It was meet that we should make merry,
and be glad: for this thy brother was dead,
and is alive again; and was lost,
and is found.
Luke 15

FATHER AND SON

The tenants in the vineyard

Jesus knew that he had only a short time in which to teach and heal.
He had many enemies among the Jewish religious leaders.
One day he told this story:

'Once there was a man who planted a vineyard, put a fence round it, dug a hole for the winepress, and built a watch-tower. Then he let out the vineyard to tenants and left home on a journey. When the time came to gather the grapes, he sent a slave to the tenants to receive from them his share of the harvest. The tenants seized the slave, beat him, and sent him back without a thing.

'Then the owner sent another slave; the tenants beat him over the head and treated him shamefully. The owner sent another slave and they killed him; and they treated many others the same way, beating some and killing others. The only one left to send was the man's own dear son.

'Last of all, then, he sent his son to the tenants.

' "I am sure they will respect my son," he said.

'But those tenants said to one another, "This is the owner's son. Come on, let's kill him, and his property will be ours!"

'So they seized the son and killed him and threw his body out of the vineyard.

'What, then, will the owner of the vineyard do?' asked Jesus. 'He will come and kill those men and hand the vineyard over to other tenants. Surely you have read this scripture?

' "The stone which the builders rejected as worthless turned out to be the most important of all." '
Mark 12

Jesus took pains to make clear his own very special relationship, as Son, to God his Father. It was a subject which aroused great anger in many of his Jewish hearers. In their eyes Jesus was guilty of blasphemy.

The healing at the pool
At the pool of Bethesda in Jerusalem Jesus healed a man who had been ill thirty-eight years. But it was the Jewish Sabbath, when all work was forbidden. And the man was caught carrying the mat on which he had been lying.

The man . . . told the Jewish authorities that it was Jesus who had healed him. So they began to persecute Jesus, because he had done this healing on a Sabbath. Jesus answered them, 'My Father is always working, and I too must work.'

This saying made the Jewish authorities all the more determined to kill him; not only had he broken the Sabbath law, but he had said that God was his own Father, and in this way had made himself equal with God.

The source of life
I am telling you the truth: whoever hears my words and believes in him who sent me has eternal life. He will not be judged, but has already passed from death to life. I am telling you the truth: the time is coming – the time has already come – when the dead will hear the voice of the Son of God, and those who hear it will come to life. Just as the Father is himself the source of life, in the same way he has made his Son to be the source of life.
John 5

'The will of him who sent me'
Everyone whom my Father gives me will come to me. I will never turn away anyone who comes to me, because I have come down from heaven to do not my own will but the will of him who sent me.
John 6

'I Am Who I Am'
If you knew me, you would know my Father also . . . You will die in your sins if you do not believe that 'I Am Who I Am' . . .
Before Abraham was born, 'I Am'.
John 8

The Father and I are one.
John 10

I am the way, the truth, and the life; no one goes to the Father except by me.
John 14

My Father has given me all things. No one knows the Son except the Father, and no one knows the Father except the Son and those to whom the Son chooses to reveal him.
Matthew 11

The people of Israel were like the tenants of a vineyard, Jesus said.

'LAZARUS, COME OUT!'

*News reached Jesus that his friend
Lazarus was very ill. Lazarus lived
in Bethany, a village just a few miles
from Jerusalem, with his two sisters,
Mary and Martha. Jesus loved them all.
The character of the sisters is caught
in the story of an earlier visit.
While Martha was rushed off her feet
making special preparations, Mary sat
listening to Jesus. But when Martha
grumbled, Jesus answered:
'Martha, Martha! You are worried and
troubled over so many things, but just one
is needed. Mary has chosen the right
thing, and it will not be taken away
from her.'*

*When Jesus heard of Lazarus' illness
he did nothing for two days. He had
aroused such antagonism that it was now
dangerous for him to go anywhere near
Jerusalem. But this was not the reason
for the delay . . .*

Jesus loved Martha and her sister and
Lazarus. Yet when he received the news that
Lazarus was ill, he stayed where he was for
two more days. Then he said to the disciples,
'Let us go back to Judaea.'

'Teacher,' the disciples answered, 'just a
short time ago the people there wanted to
stone you; are you planning to go back?'

Jesus said . . . 'Our friend Lazarus has
fallen asleep, but I will go and wake him up.'

The disciples answered, 'If he is asleep,
Lord, he will get well.'

Jesus meant that Lazarus had died, but
they thought he meant natural sleep. So Jesus
told them plainly, 'Lazarus is dead, but for
your sake I am glad that I was not with him,
so that you will believe. Let us go to him.'

Thomas (called the Twin) said to his
fellow-disciples, 'Let us all go with the
Teacher, so that we may die with him!'

When Jesus arrived, he found that Lazarus
had been buried four days before . . .

When Martha heard that Jesus was
coming, she went out to meet him, but Mary
stayed in the house.

Martha said to Jesus, 'If you had been here,
Lord, my brother would not have died! But I
know that even now God will give you
whatever you ask him for.'

'Your brother will rise to life,' Jesus told
her.

'I know,' she replied, 'that he will rise to
life on the last day.'

Jesus said to her, 'I am the resurrection and
the life. Whoever believes in me will live,
even though he dies; and whoever lives and
believes in me will never die. Do you believe
this?'

'Yes, Lord!' she answered. 'I do believe
that you are the Messiah, the Son of God,
who was to come into the world.'

After Martha said this, she went back and
called her sister Mary privately.

'The Teacher is here,' she told her, 'and is
asking for you.'

When Mary heard this, she got up and
hurried out to meet him. (Jesus had not yet
arrived in the village, but was still in the
place where Martha had met him.) The
people who were in the house with Mary,
comforting her, followed her when they saw
her get up and hurry out. They thought that
she was going to the grave to weep there.

Mary arrived where Jesus was, and as soon
as she saw him, she fell at his feet.

'Lord,' she said, 'if you had been here, my
brother would not have died!'

Jesus saw her weeping, and he saw how the people who were with her were weeping also; his heart was touched, and he was deeply moved.

'Where have you buried him?' he asked them.

'Come and see, Lord,' they answered.

Jesus wept.

'See how much he loved him!' the people said.

But some of them said, 'He gave sight to the blind, didn't he? Could he not have kept Lazarus from dying?'

Deeply moved once more, Jesus went to the tomb, which was a cave with a stone placed at the entrance.

'Take the stone away!' Jesus ordered.

Martha, the dead man's sister, answered, 'There will be a bad smell, Lord. He has been buried four days!'

Jesus said to her, 'Didn't I tell you that you would see God's glory if you believed?'

They took the stone away.

Jesus looked up and said, 'I thank you, Father, that you listen to me. I know that you always listen to me, but I say this for the sake of the people here, so that they will believe that you sent me.'

After he had said this, he called out in a loud voice, 'Lazarus, come out!'

He came out, his hands and feet wrapped in grave clothes, and with a cloth round his face.

'Untie him,' Jesus told them, 'and let him go.'

John 11

In Bethany today families still gather in the cool of the evening.

THE KING RIDES IN

'We are going up to Jerusalem, where the Son of Man will be handed over to the chief priests and teachers of the Law. They will condemn him to death and then hand him over to the Gentiles, who will mock him, whip him, and crucify him; but three days later he will be raised to life.'

Jesus was going to Jerusalem for the last time. He knew what lay ahead. And he warned his disciples what to expect.

Triumph
As they approached Jerusalem, near the towns of Bethphage and Bethany, they came to the Mount of Olives. Jesus sent two of his

disciples on ahead with these instructions:

'Go to the village there ahead of you. As soon as you get there, you will find a colt tied up that has never been ridden. Untie it and bring it here. And if someone asks you why you are doing that, tell him that the Master needs it and will send it back at once.'

So they went and found a colt out in the street, tied to the door of a house. As they were untying it, some of the bystanders asked them, 'What are you doing, untying that colt?'

They answered just as Jesus had told them, and the men let them go.

They brought the colt to Jesus, threw their cloaks over the animal, and Jesus got on. Many people spread their cloaks on the road, while others cut branches in the fields and spread them on the road. The people who were in front and those who followed behind began to shout,

'Praise God! God bless him who comes in the name of the Lord! God bless the coming kingdom of King David, our father! Praise God!'

Mark 11

Jesus weeps for the city

'Jerusalem, Jerusalem! You kill the prophets, you stone the messengers God has sent you! How many times have I wanted to put my arms round all your people, just as a hen gathers her chicks under her wings, but you would not let me! And so your Temple will be abandoned . . .'

He came closer to the city, and when he saw it, he wept over it, saying, 'If you only knew today what is needed for peace! But now you cannot see it! The time will come when your enemies will surround you with barricades, blockade you, and close in on you from every side. They will completely destroy you and the people within your walls; not a single stone will they leave in its place, because you did not recognize the time when God came to save you!'

Luke 13 and 19

Moneychangers in the Temple

When they arrived in Jerusalem, Jesus went to the Temple and began to drive out all those who were buying and selling. He overturned the tables of the money-changers and the stools of those who sold pigeons, and he would not let anyone carry anything through the temple courtyards.

He then taught the people: 'It is written in the Scriptures that God said, "My Temple will be called a house of prayer for the people of all nations." But you have turned it into a hideout for thieves!'

The chief priests and the teachers of the Law heard of this, so they began looking for some way to kill Jesus. They were afraid of him, because the whole crowd was amazed at his teaching.

When evening came, Jesus and his disciples left the city.

Mark 11

Jesus rode into the city of Jerusalem in triumph – and humility. He also wept over the city, 'because you did not recognize the time when God came to save you!'

67

THE END OF THE AGE

*Jesus had told his disciples that the
great Temple in Jerusalem would be
completely destroyed – not one stone
left standing. So they asked him to tell
them when this would happen,
and what signs there would be that the
end of the age was approaching –
the time of Jesus' return to earth
as ruler and judge.*

'Be on your guard'

Jesus answered, 'Be on your guard, and do
not let anyone deceive you. Many men,
claiming to speak for me, will come and say,
"I am the Messiah!" and they will deceive
many people. You are going to hear the noise
of battles close by and the news of battles far
away; but do not be troubled. Such things
must happen, but they do not mean that the
end has come.

'Countries will fight each other, kingdoms
will attack one another. There will be
famines and earthquakes everywhere. All
these things are like the first pains of
childbirth.

'Then you will be arrested and handed
over to be punished and be put to death. All
mankind will hate you because of me. Many
will give up their faith at that time; they will
betray one another and hate one another.
Then many false prophets will appear and
deceive many people. Such will be the
spread of evil that many people's love will
grow cold. But whoever holds out to the end
will be saved. And this Good News about the
Kingdom will be preached through all the
world for a witness to all mankind; and then
the end will come . . .

'Heaven and earth will pass away, but my
words will never pass away.

'No one knows, however, when that day
and hour will come – neither the angels in
heaven nor the Son; the Father alone
knows . . .

The final judgement

When the Son of Man comes as King and all the angels with him, he will sit on his royal throne, and the people of all the nations will be gathered before him. Then he will divide them into two groups, just as a shepherd separates the sheep from the goats. He will put the righteous people on his right and the others on his left.

Then the King will say to the people on his right, 'Come, you that are blessed by my Father! Come and possess the kingdom which has been prepared for you ever since the creation of the world. I was hungry and you fed me, thirsty and you gave me a drink; I was a stranger and you received me in your homes, naked and you clothed me; I was sick and you took care of me, in prison and you visited me.'

The righteous will then answer him, 'When, Lord, did we ever see you hungry and feed you, or thirsty and give you a drink? . . .'

The King will reply, 'I tell you, whenever you did this for one of the least important of these brothers of mine, you did it for me!'

Then he will say to those on his left, 'Away from me, you that are under God's curse! Away to the eternal fire which has been prepared for the Devil and his angels! I was hungry, but you would not feed me, thirsty but you would not give me a drink; I was a stranger but you would not welcome me in your homes, naked but you would not clothe me; I was sick and in prison but you would not take care of me.'

Matthew 25

'Be on your guard, then, because you do not know what day your Lord will come . . . you . . . must always be ready, because the Son of Man will come at an hour when you are not expecting him.'

Matthew 24

Storm clouds gather over Lake Galilee.

THE NET CLOSES

Then one of the twelve disciples – the one named Judas Iscariot – went to the chief priests and asked, 'What will you give me if I betray Jesus to you?'

They counted out thirty silver coins and gave them to him. From then on Judas was looking for a good chance to hand Jesus over to them.

Matthew 26

Jesus . . . said to his disciples, 'In two days, as you know, it will be the Passover Festival, and the Son of Man will be handed over to be crucified.

Then the chief priests and the elders met together in the palace of Caiaphas, the High Priest, and made plans to arrest Jesus secretly and put him to death.

'We must not do it during the festival,' they said, 'or the people will riot.'

The ancient temple area of the old city of Jerusalem rises above the Kidron Valley.

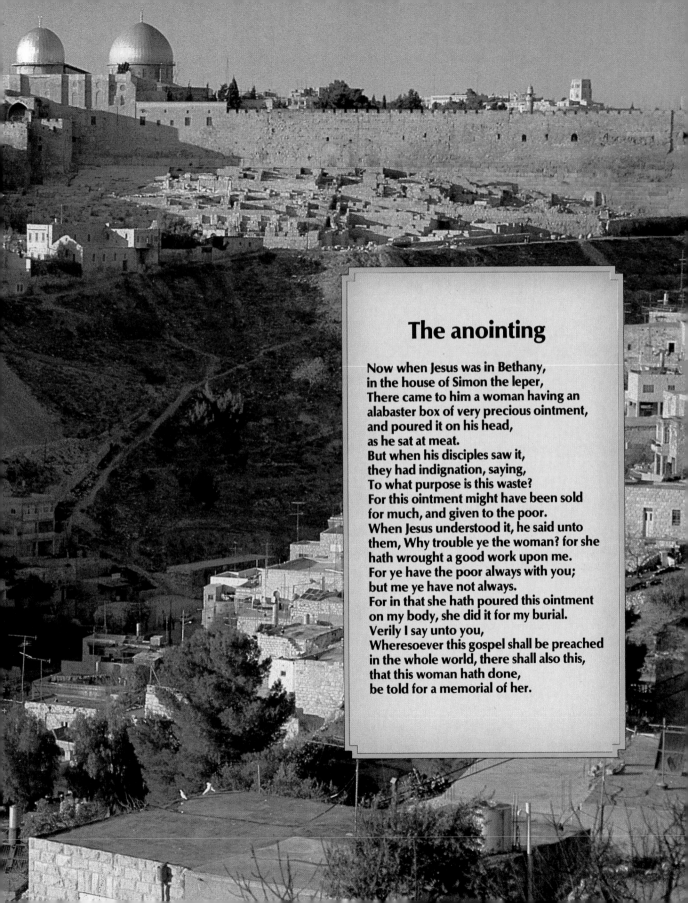

The anointing

Now when Jesus was in Bethany,
in the house of Simon the leper,
There came to him a woman having an
alabaster box of very precious ointment,
and poured it on his head,
as he sat at meat.
But when his disciples saw it,
they had indignation, saying,
To what purpose is this waste?
For this ointment might have been sold
for much, and given to the poor.
When Jesus understood it, he said unto
them, Why trouble ye the woman? for she
hath wrought a good work upon me.
For ye have the poor always with you;
but me ye have not always.
For in that she hath poured this ointment
on my body, she did it for my burial.
Verily I say unto you,
Wheresoever this gospel shall be preached
in the whole world, there shall also this,
that this woman hath done,
be told for a memorial of her.

THE LAST SUPPER

On the first day of the Festival of Unleavened Bread the disciples came to Jesus and asked him, 'Where do you want us to get the Passover meal ready for you?'

'Go to a certain man in the city,' he said to them, 'and tell him: "The Teacher says, My hour has come; my disciples and I will celebrate the Passover at your house.".'

When it was evening, Jesus and the twelve disciples sat down to eat. During the meal Jesus said, 'I tell you, one of you will betray me.'

The disciples were very upset and began to ask him, one after the other, 'Surely, Lord, you don't mean me?'

Jesus answered, 'One who dips his bread in the dish with me will betray me. The Son of Man will die as the Scriptures say he will, but how terrible for that man who betrays the Son of Man! It would have been better for that man if he had never been born!'

'This is my body'

As they were eating, Jesus took bread,
and blessed it, and brake it,
and gave it to the disciples, and said,
Take, eat; this is my body.
And he took the cup, and gave thanks,
and gave it to them, saying,
Drink ye all of it; For this
is my blood of the new testament,
which is shed for many
for the remission of sins.
Matthew 26

On the first night of the Jewish Passover, families gathered all over the crowded city to remember God's deliverance of his people.

The servant of all

Having loved his own which were in the world, he loved them unto the end. And supper being ended, the devil having now put into the heart of Judas Iscariot, Simon's son, to betray him; Jesus knowing that the Father had given all things into his hands, and that he was come from God, and went to God; He riseth from supper, and laid aside his garments; and took a towel, and girded himself. After that he poureth water into a bason, and began to wash the disciples' feet, and to wipe them with the towel wherewith he was girded . . .

. . . after he had washed their feet, and had taken his garments, and was set down again, he said unto them, Know ye what I have done to you? Ye call me Master and Lord: and ye say well; for so I am. If I then, your Lord and Master, have washed your feet; ye also ought to wash one another's feet. For I have given you an example, that ye should do as I have done to you. Verily, verily, I say unto you, The servant is not greater than his Lord; neither he that is sent greater than he that sent him. If ye know these things, happy are ye if ye do them.

John 13

COMFORT FOR JESUS' FOLLOWERS

*Judas was already on his way to arrange
the arrest of Jesus. The disciples were
unnerved by the talk of treachery,
and by Jesus' prediction that before
cock-crow loyal Peter would have denied
all knowledge of Jesus.*

A place prepared

'Do not be worried and upset,' Jesus told
them. 'Believe in God and believe also in me.
There are many rooms in my Father's house,
and I am going to prepare a place for you. I
would not tell you this if it were not so. And
after I go and prepare a place for you, I will
come back and take you to myself, so that you
will be where I am . . .'

The Helper

I am telling you the truth: whoever believes
in me will do what I do – yes, he will do even
greater things, because I am going to the
Father. And I will do whatever you ask for in
my name, so that the Father's glory will be
shown through the Son. If you ask me for
anything in my name, I will do it.

If you love me, you will obey my
commandments. I will ask the Father, and he
will give you another Helper, who will stay
with you for ever. He is the Spirit who
reveals the truth about God. The world
cannot receive him, because it cannot see
him or know him. But you know him, because
he remains with you, and is in you.

When I go, you will not be left all alone; I
will come back to you. . .

I have told you this while I am still with
you. The Helper, the Holy Spirit, whom the
Father will send in my name, will teach you
everything and make you remember all that I
have told you.

The peace of Jesus

Peace is what I leave with you; it is my own
peace that I give you. I do not give it as the
world does. Do not be worried and upset; do
not be afraid. You heard me say to you, 'I am
leaving, but I will come back to you.' If you
loved me, you would be glad that I am going
to the Father; for he is greater than I. I have
told you this now before it all happens, so
that when it does happen, you will believe. I
cannot talk with you much longer, because
the ruler of this world is coming. He has no
power over me, but the world must know that
I love the Father; that is why I do everything
as he commands me.

John 14

*On the eve of his death, in the city of Jerusalem,
Jesus reassured his closest followers.*

74

THE VINE

I am the true vine,
and my Father is the husbandman,
Every branch in me that beareth not fruit
he taketh away: and every branch
that beareth fruit, he purgeth it,
that it may bring forth more fruit.
Now ye are clean through the word
which I have spoken unto you.
Abide in me, and I in you. As the branch
cannot bear fruit of itself,
except it abide in the vine;
no more can ye except ye abide in me.
I am the vine, ye are the branches:
He that abideth in me, and I in him,
the same bringeth forth much fruit:
for without me ye can do nothing.
If a man abide not in me, he is cast
forth as a branch, and is withered;
and men gather them, and cast them
into the fire, and they are burned.
If ye abide in me, and my words abide
in you, ye shall ask what ye will,
and it shall be done unto you.
Herein is my Father glorified,
that ye bear much fruit;
so shall ye be my disciples.
John 15

The followers of Jesus are to be like branches of a vine: each grows directly from the stock, drawing its life from it and bearing fruit.

Jesus Prays for his Followers

Father, the hour has come. Give glory to your Son, so that the Son may give glory to you. For you gave him authority over all mankind, so that he might give eternal life to all those you gave him. And eternal life means knowing you, the only true God, and knowing Jesus Christ, whom you sent. I have shown your glory on earth; I have finished the work you gave me to do. Father! Give me glory in your presence now, the same glory I had with you before the world was made.

I have made you known to those you gave me out of the world. They belonged to you, and you gave them to me. They have obeyed your word, and now they know that everything you gave me comes from you. I gave them the message that you gave me, and they received it; they know that it is true that I came from you, and they believe that you sent me.

I pray for them. I do not pray for the world but for those you gave me, for they belong to you. All I have is yours, and all you have is mine; and my glory is shown through them. And now I am coming to you: I am no longer in the world, but they are in the world. Holy Father! Keep them safe by the power of your name, the name you gave me, so that they may be one just as you and I are one . . . I do not ask you to take them out of the world, but I do ask you to keep them safe from the Evil One . . .

I pray not only for them, but also for those who believe in me because of their message. I pray that they may all be one. Father! May they be in us, just as you are in me and I am in you. May they be one, so that the world will believe that you sent me.

John 17

Like this family leaving the temple area of old Jerusalem, Jesus' followers were to go out into the world, to be 'in' it if not 'of' it.

BETRAYAL

They came to a place called Gethsemane, and Jesus said to his disciples, 'Sit here while I pray.' He took Peter, James and John with him. Distress and anguish came over him, and he said to them, 'The sorrow in my heart is so great that it almost crushes me. Stay here and keep watch.'

He went a little farther on, threw himself on the ground, and prayed that, if possible, he might not have to go through that time of suffering.

'Father,' he prayed, 'my Father! All things are possible for you. Take this cup of suffering away from me. Yet not what I want, but what you want.'

Then he returned and found the three disciples asleep. He said to Peter, 'Simon, are you asleep? Weren't you able to stay awake even for one hour?' And he said to them, 'Keep watch, and pray that you will not fall into temptation. The spirit is willing, but the flesh is weak.'

He went away once more and prayed, saying the same words. Then he came back to the disciples and found them asleep; they could not keep their eyes open. And they did not know what to say to him.

When he came back a third time, he said to them, 'Are you still sleeping and resting? Enough! The hour has come! Look, the Son of Man is now being handed over to the power of sinful men. Get up, let us go. Look, here is the man who is betraying me!'

Jesus was still speaking when Judas, one of the twelve disciples, arrived. With him was a crowd armed with swords and clubs, and sent by the chief priests, the teachers of the Law, and the elders. The traitor had given the crowd a signal:

'The man I kiss is the one you want. Arrest him and take him away under guard.'

As soon as Judas arrived, he went up to Jesus and said, 'Teacher!' and kissed him. So they arrested Jesus . . .

Then all the disciples left him and ran away . . .

Then Jesus was taken to the High Priest's house, where all the chief priests, the elders, and the teachers of the Law were gathering.

Peter followed from a distance and went into the courtyard of the High Priest's house. There he sat down with the guards, keeping himself warm by the fire . . .

Peter was still down in the courtyard when one of the High Priest's servant-girls came by. When she saw Peter warming himself, she looked straight at him and said, 'You, too, were with Jesus of Nazareth.'

But he denied it.

'I don't know . . . I don't understand what you are talking about,' he answered, and went out into the passage. Just then a cock crowed.

The servant-girl saw him there and began to repeat to the bystanders, 'He is one of them!'

But Peter denied it again.

A little while later the bystanders accused Peter again, 'You can't deny that you are one of them, because you, too, are from Galilee.'

Then Peter said, 'I swear that I am telling the truth! May God punish me if I am not! I do not know the man you are talking about!'

Just then a cock crowed a second time, and Peter remembered how Jesus had said to him, 'Before the cock crows twice, you will say three times that you do not know me.'

And he broke down and cried.

Mark 14

Across the Kidron Valley from the old city of Jerusalem the gnarled, ancient olive-trees are silent reminders of the anguish of Jesus as he faced the reality of dying for the sin of the world.

ON TRIAL

Jesus' accusers were out for his blood. But under the Roman occupation the Jews were not allowed to carry out a sentence of death. So Jesus stood trial first before the Jewish Council, then he was taken to the Roman governor . . .

Jesus before the Jewish Council

The chief priests and the whole Council tried to find some false evidence against Jesus to put him to death; but they could not find any, even though many people came forward and told lies about him. Finally two men stepped up and said, 'This man said, "I am able to tear down God's Temple and three days later build it up again." '

The High Priest stood up and said to Jesus, 'Have you no answer to give to this accusation against you?' But Jesus kept quiet. Again the High Priest spoke to him, 'In the name of the living God I now put you on oath: tell us if you are the Messiah, the Son of God.'

Jesus answered him, 'So you say. But I tell all of you: from this time on you will see the Son of Man sitting on the right hand of the Almighty and coming on the clouds of heaven!'

At this the High Priest tore his clothes and said, 'Blasphemy! We don't need any more witnesses! You have just heard his blasphemy! What do you think?'

They answered, 'He is guilty and must die.'

Then they spat in his face and beat him; and those who slapped him said, 'Prophesy for us, Messiah! Guess who hit you!'

Matthew 26

Jesus before Pilate

The whole group rose up and took Jesus before Pilate, where they began to accuse him:

'We caught this man misleading our people, telling them not to pay taxes to the Emperor and claiming that he himself is the Messiah, a king.'

Pilate asked him, 'Are you the king of the Jews?'

'So you say,' answered Jesus.

Then Pilate said to the chief priests and the crowds, 'I find no reason to condemn this man.'

But they insisted even more strongly, 'With his teaching he is starting a riot among the people all through Judaea. He began in Galilee and now has come here.'

Luke 23

Jesus before King Herod

When Pilate heard this, he asked, 'Is this man a Galilean?'

When he learnt that Jesus was from the region ruled by Herod, he sent him to Herod, who was also in Jerusalem at that time.

Herod was very pleased when he saw Jesus, because he had heard about him and had been wanting to see him for a long time. He was hoping to see Jesus perform some miracle. So Herod asked Jesus many questions, but Jesus made no answer.

The chief priests and the teachers of the Law stepped forward and made strong accusations against Jesus.

Herod and his soldiers mocked Jesus and treated him with contempt; then they put a fine robe on him and sent him back to Pilate. On that very day Herod and Pilate became friends; before this they had been enemies.

Luke 23

Sentenced to death

At every Passover Festival the Roman governor was in the habit of setting free any one prisoner the crowd asked for. At that time there was a well-known prisoner named Jesus Barabbas. So when the crowd gathered, Pilate asked them, 'Which one do you want me to set free for you? Jesus Barabbas or Jesus called the Messiah?' He knew very well that the Jewish authorities had handed Jesus over to him because they were jealous.

While Pilate was sitting in the judgement hall, his wife sent him a message: 'Have nothing to do with that innocent man, because in a dream last night I suffered much on account of him.'

The chief priests and the elders persuaded the crowd to ask Pilate to set Barabbas free and have Jesus put to death. But Pilate asked the crowd, 'Which one of these two do you want me to set free for you?'

'Barabbas!' they answered.

'What, then, shall I do with Jesus called the Messiah?' Pilate asked them.

'Crucify him!' they all answered.

But Pilate asked, 'What crime has he committed?'

Then they started shouting at the top of their voices, 'Crucify him!'

When Pilate saw that it was no use to go on, but that a riot might break out, he took some water, washed his hands in front of the crowd, and said, 'I am not responsible for the death of this man! This is your doing!'

The whole crowd answered, 'Let the punishment for his death fall on us and our children!'

Then Pilate set Barabbas free for them; and after he had Jesus whipped, he handed him over to be crucified.

Matthew 27

In a rigged trial Jesus was hurried from the Jewish to the Roman authorities, so that his execution could be carried out before the Passover Festival began.

'FATHER, FORGIVE THEM'

As they were going out, they met a man from Cyrene named Simon, and the soldiers forced him to carry Jesus' cross. They came to a place called Golgotha, which means 'The Place of the Skull'. There they offered Jesus wine mixed with a bitter substance; but after tasting it, he would not drink it.

They crucified him and then divided his clothes among them by throwing dice. After that they sat there and watched him. Above his head they put the written notice of the accusation against him:

'This is Jesus, the King of the Jews.'

Then they crucified two bandits with Jesus, one on his right and the other on his left.

People passing by shook their heads and hurled insults at Jesus:

'You were going to tear down the Temple and build it up again in three days! Save yourself if you are God's Son! Come on down from the cross!'

In the same way the chief priests and the teachers of the Law and the elders jeered at him.

'He saved others, but he cannot save himself! Isn't he the king of Israel? If he comes down off the cross now, we will believe in him! He trusts in God and claims to be God's Son. Well, then, let us see if God wants to save him now!'

Even the bandits who had been crucified with him insulted him in the same way.

At noon the whole country was covered with darkness which lasted for three hours.
Matthew 27

Then Pilate's soldiers took Jesus into the governor's palace, and the whole company gathered round him. They stripped off his clothes and put a scarlet robe on him. Then they made a crown out of thorny branches and placed it on his head, and put a stick in his right hand; then they knelt before him and mocked him.

'Long live the King of the Jews!' they said. They spat on him, and took the stick and hit him over the head. When they had finished mocking him, they took the robe off and put his own clothes back on him. Then they led him out to crucify him.

Jesus was crucified on a rocky outcrop shaped like a skull. Darkness covered the land for three hours.

Jesus' words from the cross

Jesus cried with a loud voice, saying Eli, Eli,
lama sabachthani? that is to say,
My God, my God, why hast thou forsaken
me?
Matthew 27

Then said Jesus, Father, forgive them;
for they know not what they do.

And one of the malefactors which were
hanged railed on him, saying,
If thou be Christ, save thyself and us.
But the other answering rebuked him,
saying, Dost thou not fear God,
seeing thou art in the same condemnation?
And we indeed justly; for we receive
the due reward of our deeds:
but this man hath done nothing amiss.
And he said unto Jesus,
Lord, remember me
when thou comest into thy kingdom.
And Jesus said unto him,
Verily I say unto thee,
Today shalt thou be with me in paradise.
Luke 23

Now there stood by the cross of Jesus
his mother and his mother's sister,

Mary the wife of Cleophas,
and Mary Magdalene.
When Jesus therefore saw his mother,
and the disciple standing by,
whom he loved,
he saith unto his mother,
Woman, behold thy son!
Then saith he to the disciple,
Behold thy mother!
And from that hour that disciple
took her unto his own home.
After this, Jesus knowing that all things
were now accomplished, that the
scripture might be fulfilled,
saith, I thirst.
Now there was set a vessel full of vinegar:
and they filled a spunge with vinegar,
and put it upon hyssop,
and put it to his mouth.
When Jesus therefore had received
the vinegar, he said, It is finished.
John 19

And when Jesus had cried with a loud
voice, he said, Father,
into thy hands I commend my spirit:
and having said thus, he gave up the ghost.
Luke 23

Tomb in the Rock

Then the Jewish authorities asked Pilate to allow them to break the legs of the men who had been crucified, and to take the bodies down from the crosses. They requested this because it was Friday, and they did not want the bodies to stay on the crosses on the Sabbath, since the coming Sabbath was especially holy.

So the soldiers went and broke the legs of the first man and then of the other man who had been crucified with Jesus. But when they came to Jesus, they saw that he was already dead, so they did not break his legs.

One of the soldiers, however, plunged his spear into Jesus' side, and at once blood and water poured out. (The one who saw this happen has spoken of it, so that you also may believe. What he said is true, and he knows that he speaks the truth.) This was done to make the scripture come true:

'Not one of his bones will be broken.'
And there is another scripture that says, 'People will look at him whom they pierced.'

After this, Joseph, who was from the town of Arimathea, asked Pilate if he could take Jesus' body. (Joseph was a follower of Jesus, but in secret, because he was afraid of the Jewish authorities.) Pilate told him he could have the body, so Joseph went and took it away.

Nicodemus, who at first had gone to see Jesus at night, went with Joseph, taking with him about thirty kilogrammes of spices, a mixture of myrrh and aloes.

The two men took Jesus' body and wrapped it in linen with the spices according to the Jewish custom of preparing a body for burial. There was a garden in the place where Jesus had been put to death, and in it there was a new tomb where no one had ever been buried. Since it was the day before the Sabbath and because the tomb was close by, they placed Jesus' body there.
John 19

The guard

The next day, which was a Sabbath, the chief priests and the Pharisees met with Pilate and said, 'Sir, we remember that while that liar was still alive he said, "I will be raised to life three days later." Give orders, then, for his tomb to be carefully guarded until the third day, so that his disciples will not be able to go and steal the body, and then tell people that he was raised from death. This last lie would be even worse than the first one.'

'Take a guard,' Pilate told them; 'go and make the tomb as secure as you can.'

So they left and made the tomb secure by putting a seal on the stone and leaving the guard on watch.
Matthew 27

This first-century rock tomb was sealed with a great stone rolled across the entrance.

THE LORD IS RISEN!

In the end of the sabbath, as it began
to dawn toward the first day of the week,
came Mary Magdalene and the other Mary
to see the sepulchre. And, behold,
there was a great earthquake:
for the angel of the Lord descended
from heaven, and came and rolled back
the stone from the door, and sat upon it.
His countenance was like lightning,
and his raiment white as snow:
And for fear of him the keepers did shake,
and became as dead men.
And the angel answered and said unto
the women, Fear not ye: for I know that
ye seek Jesus, which was crucified.
He is not here: for he is risen, as he said.
Come, see the place where the Lord lay.
And go quickly, and tell his disciples
that he is risen from the dead . . .

Now when they were going, behold,
some of the watch came into the city,
and shewed unto the chief priests
all the things that were done.
And when they were assembled with
the elders, and had taken counsel,
they gave large money unto the soldiers,
Saying, Say ye, His disciples came by night,
and stole him away while we slept.
And if this come to the governor's ears,
we will persuade him, and secure you.
Matthew 28

Peter and John

Mary Magdalene . . . went running to Simon Peter and the other disciple, whom Jesus loved, and told them, 'They have taken the Lord from the tomb, and we don't know where they have put him!'

Then Peter and the other disciple went to the tomb. The two of them were running, but the other disciple ran faster than Peter and reached the tomb first. He bent over and saw the linen wrappings, but he did not go in.

Behind him came Simon Peter, and he went straight into the tomb. He saw the linen wrappings lying there and the cloth which had been round Jesus' head. It was not lying with the linen wrappings but was rolled up by itself.

Then the other disciple, who had reached the tomb first, also went in; he saw and believed. (They still did not understand the scripture which said that he must rise from death.)

Then the disciples went back home.
John 20

Mary

Mary stood crying outside the tomb. While she was still crying, she bent over and looked in the tomb and saw two angels there dressed in white, sitting where the body of Jesus had been, one at the head and the other at the feet.

'Woman, why are you crying?' they asked her.

She answered, 'They have taken my Lord away, and I do not know where they have put him!'

Then she turned round and saw Jesus standing there; but she did not know that it was Jesus.

'Woman, why are you crying?' Jesus asked

her. 'Who is it that you are looking for?'

She thought he was the gardener, so she said to him, 'If you took him away, sir, tell me where you have put him, and I will go and get him.'

Jesus said to her, 'Mary!'

She turned towards him and said in Hebrew, 'Rabboni!' (This means 'Teacher'.)

'Do not hold on to me,' Jesus told her, 'because I have not yet gone back up to the Father. But go to my brothers and tell them that I am returning to him who is my Father and their Father, my God and their God.'

So Mary Magdalene went and told the disciples that she had seen the Lord and related to them what he had told her.

John 20

The great stone had been rolled away . . . The body of Jesus had gone.

HE IS RISEN INDEED!

On that same day two of Jesus' followers were going to a village named Emmaus, about eleven kilometres from Jerusalem, and they were talking to each other about all the things that had happened.

As they talked and discussed, Jesus himself drew near and walked along with them; they saw him, but somehow did not recognize him.

Jesus said to them, 'What are you talking about to each other, as you walk along?'

They stood still, with sad faces. One of them, named Cleopas, asked him, 'Are you the only visitor in Jerusalem who doesn't know the things that have been happening there these last few days?'

'What things?' he asked.

'The things that happened to Jesus of Nazareth,' they answered. 'This man was a prophet and was considered by God and by all the people to be powerful in everything he said and did. Our chief priests and rulers handed him over to be sentenced to death, and he was crucified. And we had hoped that he would be the one who was going to set Israel free.

'Besides all that, this is now the third day since it happened. Some of the women of our group surprised us; they went at dawn to the tomb, but could not find his body. They came back saying they had seen a vision of angels who told them that he is alive. Some of our group went to the tomb and found it exactly as the women had said, but they did not see him.'

Then Jesus said to them, 'How foolish you are, how slow you are to believe everything the prophets said! Was it not necessary for the Messiah to suffer these things and then to enter his glory?' And Jesus explained to them what was said about himself in all the Scriptures, beginning with the books of Moses and the writings of all the prophets.

As they came near the village to which they were going, Jesus acted as if he were going farther; but they held him back, saying, 'Stay with us; the day is almost over and it is getting dark.'

So he went in to stay with them. He sat down to eat with them, took the bread, and said the blessing; then he broke the bread and gave it to them. Then their eyes were opened and they recognized him, but he disappeared from their sight.

They said to each other, 'Wasn't it like a fire burning in us when he talked to us on the road and explained the Scriptures to us?'

They got up at once and went back to Jerusalem, where they found the eleven disciples gathered together with the others and saying, 'The Lord is risen indeed! He has appeared to Simon!'

The two then explained to them what had happened on the road, and how they had recognized the Lord when he broke the bread.

While the two were telling them this, suddenly the Lord himself stood among them and said to them, 'Peace be with you.'

They were terrified, thinking that they were seeing a ghost. But he said to them, 'Why are you alarmed? Why are these doubts coming up in your minds? Look at my hands and my feet, and see that it is I myself. Feel me, and you will know, for a ghost doesn't have flesh and bones, as you can see I have.'

He said this and showed them his hands and his feet. They still could not believe, they were so full of joy and wonder; so he asked them, 'Have you anything here to eat?'

They gave him a piece of cooked fish, which he took and ate in their presence.

Then he said to them, 'These are the very things I told you about while I was still with you: everything written about me in the Law of Moses, the writings of the prophets, and the Psalms had to come true.'

Then he opened their minds to understand the Scriptures, and said to them, 'This is what is written: the Messiah must suffer and must rise from death three days later, and in his name the message about repentance and the forgiveness of sins must be preached to all nations, beginning in Jerusalem. You are witnesses of these things.'

Luke 24

Thomas

One of the twelve disciples, Thomas (called the Twin), was not with them when Jesus came. So the other disciples told him, 'We have seen the Lord!'

Thomas said to them, 'Unless I see the scars of the nails in his hands and put my finger on those scars and my hand in his side, I will not believe.'

A week later the disciples were together again indoors, and Thomas was with them. The doors were locked, but Jesus came and stood among them and said, 'Peace be with you!'

Then he said to Thomas, 'Put your finger here, and look at my hands; then stretch out your hand and put it in my side. Stop your doubting, and believe!'

Thomas answered him, 'My Lord and my God!'

Jesus said to him, 'Do you believe because you see me? How happy are those who believe without seeing me!'

John 20

Shattered, disillusioned, disciples of Jesus were walking to Emmaus (LEFT) when they were joined by a stranger . . . The great doorway of the Church of the Holy Sepulchre symbolizes the fact that the death and resurrection of Jesus opened the door to a new life for all who will come to God through him.

'MY WITNESSES'

After this, Jesus appeared once more to his disciples at Lake Tiberias. This is how it happened . . .

Simon Peter said to the others, 'I am going fishing.'

'We will come with you,' they told him. So they went out in a boat, but all that night they did not catch a thing. As the sun was rising, Jesus stood at the water's edge, but the disciples did not know that it was Jesus.

Then he asked them, 'Young men, haven't you caught anything?'

'Not a thing,' they answered.

He said to them, 'Throw your net out on the right side of the boat, and you will catch some.'

So they threw the net and could not pull it back in, because they had caught so many fish.

The disciple whom Jesus loved said to Peter, 'It is the Lord!' When Peter heard that it was the Lord, he wrapped his outer garment round him (for he had taken his clothes off) and jumped into the water.

The other disciples came to shore in the boat, pulling the net full of fish. They were not very far from land, about a hundred metres away. When they stepped ashore, they saw a charcoal fire there with fish on it and some bread.

Then Jesus said to them, 'Bring some of the fish you have just caught.'

Simon Peter went aboard and dragged the net ashore full of big fish, a hundred and fifty-three in all; even though there were so many, still the net did not tear.

Jesus said to them, 'Come and eat.'

None of the disciples dared ask him, 'Who are you?' because they knew it was the Lord. So Jesus went over, took the bread, and gave it to them; he did the same with the fish.

This, then, was the third time Jesus appeared to the disciples after he was raised from death.

John 21

Jesus and Peter

After they had eaten, Jesus said to Simon Peter, 'Simon son of John, do you love me more than these others do?'

'Yes, Lord,' he answered, 'you know that I love you.'

Jesus said to him, 'Take care of my lambs.'

A second time Jesus said to him, 'Simon son of John, do you love me?'

'Yes, Lord,' he answered, 'you know that I love you.'

Jesus said to him, 'Take care of my sheep.'

A third time Jesus said, 'Simon son of John, do you love me?'

Peter was sad because Jesus asked him the third time, 'Do you love me?' so he said to him, 'Lord, you know everything; you know that I love you!'

Jesus said to him, 'Take care of my sheep.'

John 21

Jesus appeared to his followers on many occasions, some of them beside Lake Galilee, scene of so much of his teaching and healing. His followers were to be witnesses to him 'to the end of the age'.

Jesus' last words

Jesus came and spake unto the disciples,
saying, All power is given unto me
in heaven and in earth.
Go ye therefore, and teach all nations,
baptizing them in the name of the Father,
and of the Son, and of the Holy Ghost:
Teaching them to observe all things
whatsoever I have commanded you:
and lo, I am with you alway,
even unto the end of the world.
Matthew 28

Ye shall receive power, after that
the Holy Ghost is come upon you:
and ye shall be witnesses unto me
both in Jerusalem,
and in all Judaea, and in Samaria,
and unto the uttermost part of the earth.
And when he had spoken these things,
while they beheld, he was taken up;
and a cloud received him
out of their sight.
And while they looked stedfastly toward
heaven as he went up, behold, two men
stood by them in white apparel;
Which also said, Ye men of Galilee,
why stand ye gazing up into heaven?
this same Jesus, which is taken up from
you into heaven, shall so come
in like manner as ye have seen him
go into heaven.
Then returned they unto Jerusalem
from the mount called Olivet.
Acts 1

In his disciples' presence Jesus performed many other miracles which are not written down in this book. But these have been written in order that you may believe that Jesus is the Messiah, the Son of God, and that through your faith in him you may have life.

John 20